DO YOU KNOW?

Level 1

BIRDS AND INSECTS

Inspired by BBC Earth TV series and developed with input from BBC Earth natural history specialists

Written by Alex Woolf
Text adapted by Jennifer Dobson
Series Editor: Nick Coates

LADYBIRD BOOKS

UK | USA | Canada | Ireland | Australia
India | New Zealand | South Africa

Ladybird Books is part of the Penguin Random House group of companies
whose addresses can be found at global.penguinrandomhouse.com.
www.penguin.co.uk   www.puffin.co.uk   www.ladybird.co.uk

Penguin
Random House
UK

First published 2020
001

Contents

New words

beak

dance
(verb)

feather

grow

hatch

honey

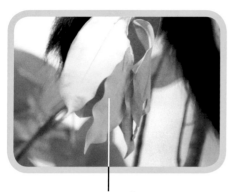

leaf
(leaves)

light
(noun)

mate
(noun)

seed

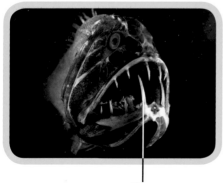

tooth
(teeth)

wing

What is a bird?

Birds are animals.
They have **feathers**
and **wings**.

They do not have **teeth**.
They have a **beak**.

This puffin's beak has lots of colours.

All birds lay eggs. The babies **grow** in the eggs.

Then, they **hatch**.

FIND OUT!

Use books or the internet to find out what the biggest bird in the world is. What is the smallest?

What is an insect?

An insect is a small animal.

An insect's body has three parts.

Insects have six legs.

This atlas moth is a big insect.

Lots of insects have wings and can fly.

 **THINK!**

Is a spider an insect? Why? Why not?

Where do birds and insects live?

Many birds make nests.

nest

This drongo makes its nest from parts of trees.

Weaver ants make homes from **leaves**.

Termites make very big homes.

These wasps are making their nest.

▶ WATCH!

Watch the video (see page 32).
What does the ant larva make
to help the ants build their home?
Is it dirt, honey or silk?

Who do insects live with?

A lot of insects do not live with other insects.

This stick insect does not live with others.

Some insects live in homes with others.

Ants live in big homes with many other ants.

They all do jobs.

Honeybees live with other honeybees.

THINK!

How many people do you live with?

Do all birds fly?

Ostriches are birds, but they cannot fly. They can run very fast.

Penguins cannot fly. They can walk, and they can swim.

 **PROJECT**

Work in a group.
Make a poster about ostriches and penguins.
Find out where they live.
Draw a map of the world.
Draw or stick pictures of the birds on
the parts of the world where they live.

What do birds eat?

Some birds eat fruit and seeds.

nectar

Hummingbirds have long beaks. They drink nectar from flowers.

Some birds eat small animals.

Some birds catch insects.

These birds take eggs. Then, they eat the eggs.

WATCH!

Watch the video (see page 32).
How many times a day must this hummingbird drink?

What do insects eat?

Insects eat plants, leaves and other insects.

The grasscutter ant makes food from grass.

This dragonfly eats moths.

The praying mantis catches insects with its legs.

Locusts eat plants.

📖 FIND OUT!

Use books or the internet to find out what a dung beetle eats.

How do birds find mates?

Some birds sing for a **mate**.

Some birds show lots of colours.

Birds of paradise **dance**.

Jackson's widowbirds jump.

The bowerbird makes a big home.

▶ **WATCH!**

Watch the video (see page 32).
What does the bowerbird make its home out of?

How do insects find mates?

Some insects show a **light**.
Some make noises.

Fireflies make a light.

Crickets make noises.

Some butterflies dance.

FIND OUT!

Use books or the internet to find out how crickets make a noise.

What do we know about baby birds?

Baby birds come from eggs.
Many baby birds cannot fly.

These king penguins get food for their babies.

This baby sandgrouse drinks water from its father's feathers.

These barnacle goose babies are very small.

FIND OUT!

Use books or the internet to find out the name for a baby bird.

What do we know about young insects?

A baby insect is called a larva.

larva

1. This caterpillar is the larva of a moth.

2. Now it is a pupa.

moth

pupa

3. Its body changes.
Now it is a moth.

LOOK!

Look at the pages.
When does this insect get wings?

Can birds and insects help us?

Some insects eat our food.
Birds eat these insects.

The American redstart eats these insects. There is more food for us.

Butterflies help plants and flowers. We can eat some of the plants and flowers.

Honeybees make **honey**. We can eat the honey.

FIND OUT!

Honeybees make honey. **Use books or the internet** to find out which insects make silk.

Quiz

Choose the correct answers.

1 Birds have feathers,
wings and . . .
   a a beak.
   b teeth.

2 Insects have . . .
   a four legs.
   b six legs.

3 Penguins and
ostriches . . .
   a can fly.
   b can't fly.

4 Hummingbirds have
long beaks to . . .
  a drink from flowers.
  b catch insects.

5 A baby insect is
called a . . .
  a chick.
  b larva.

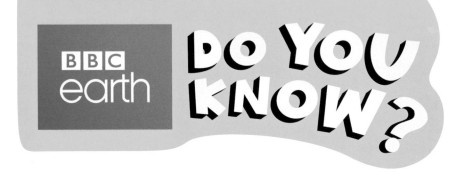

BBC earth **DO YOU KNOW?**

**Visit www.ladybirdeducation.co.uk for
FREE DO YOU KNOW? teaching resources.**

- video clips with simplified voiceover and subtitles
- video and comprehension activities
- class projects and lesson plans
- audio recording of every book
- digital version of every book
- full answer keys

**To access video clips, audio tracks and
digital books:**

1 Go to **www.ladybirdeducation.co.uk**
2 Click "Unlock book"
3 Enter the code below

4XhI89lpcP

**Stay safe online! Some of the DO YOU KNOW? activities ask
children to do extra research online. Remember:**

- ensure an adult is supervising;
- use established search engines such as Google or Kiddle;
- children should never share personal details, such as name,
  home or school address, telephone number or photos.